BRITAIN IN OLD PHOTOGRAPHS

LINCOLN CATHEDRAL

DAVID CUPPLEDITCH

SUTTON PUBLISHING LIMITED

Sutton Publishing Limited
Phoenix Mill · Far Thrupp · Stroud
Gloucestershire · GL5 2BU

First published 1996

Copyright © David Cuppleditch, 1996

British Library Cataloguing in Publication Data
A catalogue record for this book is available from the
British Library.

ISBN 0-7509-0700-2

Typeset in 10/12 Perpetua.
Typesetting and origination by
Alan Sutton Publishing Limited.
Printed in Great Britain by
Ebenezer Baylis, Worcester.

Lincoln Cathedral from the Eastgate Hotel, showing the Cathedral School in the foreground to the right.

CONTENTS

Introduction   7

1. Cathedral Images   9

2. Around the Cathedral   25

3. Cathedral People   53

4. Maintenance & Restoration   83

5. Events   105

    Acknowledgements   126

'Carols at Lincoln' by Jack McCarthy. This painting adorned the front cover of *Readers Digest* in December 1972. Twenty-nine million copies in thirteen different languages were published.

INTRODUCTION

Lincoln Cathedral is thought by many to be the foremost cathedral in England, on account of its superb location as well as its magnificent and harmonious design, and finely carved decoration.

Despite its tranquil atmosphere, which can make a visitor feel that the building must have existed unchanging and peaceful for centuries, the cathedral has had a turbulent past. From the time of Remigius, the first bishop, appointed by William the Conqueror in 1067, controversy was never far away. The second bishop, Robert Bloet, was described as a 'most profligate, indolent and licentious man'. When he died at Woodstock, Oxfordshire, in 1123, he was disembowelled; his bowels embalmed and interred at Eynsham monastery, while his body was conveyed to Lincoln for burial. In 1185 there was a tremendous earthquake in Lincoln that cleft the cathedral in two. The man responsible for rebuilding much of it was Hugh of Avalon, a very great architect as well as a reverent churchman. But even Bishop Hugh, the only Bishop of Lincoln ever to become a saint, was not averse to unimaginable acts. When visiting a French monastery he is reputed to have gnawed two fingers from the mummified hand of Mary Magdalene, much to the disgust of the assembled monks, just to secure them for Lincoln. After St Hugh's death his head was separated from his body: the body was displayed in a bejewelled chest in one part of the cathedral while his head, which was placed in a gold and silver coffer, was in another. In 1364 two robbers stole the head, even though a watch was being kept. They threw away the skull, sold the coffer in London and were themselves robbed as they returned to Lincoln. Eventually they were hanged for their crime.

The violent-tempered Dean Mackworth used to march armed men into meetings in the cathedral in the 1430s; they acted as his bodyguards. Then there was Cardinal Wolsey: appointed dean in 1509, he served as bishop for about six months in 1514. He was an arrogant and avaricious man whose ambition it was to seize the papal throne. It was his harsh and cruel policies that sparked off the Lincolnshire Rebellion of 1536. This uprising of 25,000 men reached the cathedral chapter house before dispersing. Most of the ringleaders, who included the vicar of Louth, were hanged, drawn and quartered.

By the end of Henry VIII's reign there had been so much pilfering and damage in the cathedral that 'few possessions of value appear to have survived'. In 1548 Bishop Holbech and Dean George Henage rampaged through the cathedral, defacing nearly all the tombs. But even worse was to come in the Civil War, when zealot roundheads ripped up over 200 brasses from the floor and removed the brass gates that led to the choir. Later, in 1727, there was a riot in the city when attempts to remove the timber spires on the west front incensed Lincolnians. The towers were eventually removed in 1807, when they had become unsafe.

The trials of Bishop Edward King in 1889 and 1890 seem tame in the light of previous events. The Church Association complained to the Archbishop of Canterbury that they did not approve of his practices: for example, his way of celebrating the Eucharist – using lighted candles on the altar and mixing water with sacramental wine.

Then we come to the twentieth century with its monumental problems concerning the repair and preservation of the cathedral. Most of these problems stemmed from the 1185 earthquake, but the more recent concerns of dry rot and acid rain (and pollution in general) made matters even more complicated. Fundraising on a scale not previously envisaged became the order of the day, and the Lincoln clergy were placed under greater and greater pressure to undertake this task. Such champions as Dean Fry, Bishop Dunlop, Canon Cook, Canon Peter Binnall and Dean Oliver Fiennes all played an important part in this, providing good ideas and sound leadership.

More recently, and outside the scope of a book entitled *Lincoln Cathedral in Old Photographs*, there have been problems at Lincoln Cathedral, with poor financial decisions and clashes of personality both playing their part. Money and confidence have both been lost – but one hopes that time will heal the wounds, and that this great cathedral will enter the new millennium renewed and strengthened.

CATHEDRAL IMAGES

Before the advent of photography images of Lincoln Cathedral were largely depicted in prints and paintings. This print appeared in an issue of the Gentleman's Magazine *dating from 1822.*

Probably the most reproduced image has been John Wilson Carmichael's 'The Brayford Pool and Lincoln Cathedral', painted in 1858.

William Callow's 1853 painting of the cathedral from High Street shows just how much the buildings have changed.

The artist most associated with views of Lincoln is undoubtedly Peter de Wint (1784–1849). The Usher Art Gallery houses a comprehensive collection of his paintings. This is de Wint's view of Lincoln Cathedral from Drury Lane.

Even lesser artists such as Max Hofler have found inspiration in Lincoln.

A hitherto unknown artist named Ernest Vickers produced this delightful view of Lincoln, which featured on a postcard in the 'Lincoln Imp' series.

Another prolific Edwardian postcard artist was Arthur C. Payne (1856–1933), who completed a series of Lincoln cards. This was entitled 'The Minster from Broadgate'.

Of the moderns Lowry's style was quite unique. When the artist (1887–1976) visited Lincoln in 1950 to complete some preliminary sketches for this painting he omitted the cathedral altogether, only to add it at a later date.

Rowland Hilder's vision of Lincoln was much more sympathetic. Hilder (1906–93) dealt with the Brayford in a much more traditional manner.

Lincoln was fortunate enough to escape any serious damage during the Second World War. Secret plans made by the Luftwaffe revealed years later that the city had been on their hit-list, primarily because of Ruston's engineering works.

If the cathedral had been bombed it would have negated the entire painstaking restoration of 1920–32.

An aerial view of the cathedral, 1950s. The cathedral and castle provide a strong contrast with the industrial housing beyond.

The cathedral's ground plan may be seen clearly here, from the twin towers of the west front to the distinctive chapter house.

One of the most charming views of the cathedral is from Vicars' Court, as the presence of these artists testifies. The photograph was taken in about 1955.

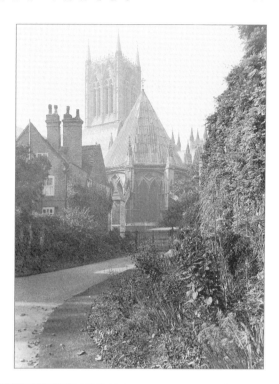

This view is from the Priory, which later became the residence of Sir Francis Hill.

This photograph, looking towards Vicars' Court, clearly shows the tithe barn in the foreground before renovation.

High Street, *c.* 1900. The cathedral, with its imposing position high above the city, has dominated this scene for centuries.

Lincoln in the snow, 1940s. This beautifully composed photograph was taken from the back of the Adam & Eve public house.

Exchequergate, late nineteenth century. This was the main way into the cathedral precincts from the west. There were two pubs here, one of which was Great Tom Inn (named after the cathedral bell), and they were once very popular.

Postcards like this were produced in their thousands. Vicars' Court has pride of place in the centre, while the other views are (clockwise from top left) as follows: Potter Gate and the cathedral tower; the Jew's House on Steep Hill, which dates from the twelfth century and is among the oldest examples of domestic architecture in this country; the thirteenth-century chapter house; and the Chancery, to the east of the cathedral.

This photograph of Lincoln from the Brayford was taken by Peter Sharp of Studio 7. Not only does it portray the cathedral but also the city as future generations will see it from the new University of Lincolnshire.

AROUND THE CATHEDRAL

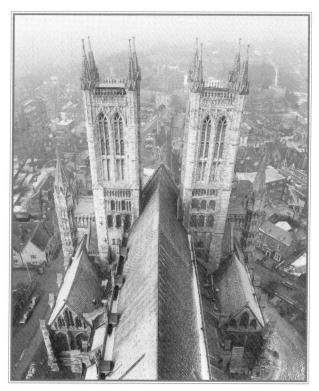

In this view it is possible to see how the cathedral dominates the city.
The western towers are 206 ft high.

Bishop Alnwick's tower, to the east of Edward King House. William of Alnwick was bishop from 1436 to 1449. In 1954 the Ministry of Public Buildings and Works took over the tower; it is now in the care of English Heritage. The tower is open to the public on certain days.

This is how the west front is supposed to have looked in Norman times just before the earthquake of 1185, which destroyed much of the Norman cathedral.

The imposing Norman west front. Over the door is a set of eleven seated statues of crowned kings, the work of Treasurer de Welbourne (*c.* 1370). They commence with William the Conqueror and end with Edward III. Two kings were crowned in the cathedral, Stephen (in 1135) and Henry II (in 1154).

Looking towards the south transept, completed in the early thirteenth century. The famous Bishop's Eye rose window still has its original early fourteenth-century stained glass. This was removed for safe-keeping during the Second World War, and was replaced undamaged in 1948.

St Anne's chapel. The statue of St Anne teaching the Blessed Virgin Mary to read is in the centre of the photograph.

The morning chapel is on the north side of the nave, at the west end. The Constance Howard passion frontal can be seen in this photograph, together with benches designed by Laurence Bond.

The Longland chapel is a simple and unpretentious chapel on the west of the south door. It was named after John Longland, bishop from 1521 to 1547. He was chancellor of Oxford University, and does not seem to have been very popular there: on one occasion he was pelted with stones.

The cathedral roof during releading, August 1964.

The central tower is 271 ft tall. This stunning photograph clearly shows the arcading and vaulting. The cathedral's famous bell, 'Great Tom of Lincoln' – which weighs 5½ tons – was hauled up into the tower through the circular hole visible at the top left of the picture.

High up in the south-west tower is the ringing chamber.

From the outside this western tower looks splendid as it frames the observatory tower of Lincoln Castle.

But from the inside, looking up to the ringing chamber (a view people rarely see), the use of reinforced concrete becomes apparent, supporting the structure of the tower. This work dates from the 1920s, when Robert Godfrey, cathedral surveyor, managed to stop serious deterioration of the cathedral's fabric.

The chapter house is one of the earliest polygonal chapter houses in England, dating from the early thirteenth century. Its ten sides are supported by extravagant flying buttresses. The building was restored in Victorian times by the architect to the Dean and Chapter, J.L. Pearson RA.

Few people realise that there is a prison in the cathedral. Known as 'La Wynde', it is situated in the north-west tower and to this day can only be reached by ladder. It was rediscovered in 1785, and was used to house unruly lay-vicars or rebellious sub-deans.

The chapter library is situated over the cloisters. Part of the medieval library burnt down in 1609, and the present colonnade and gallery were built by Sir Christopher Wren in 1674. The library was built primarily to house the remarkable collection of books and manuscripts acquired by Dean Honywood during his exile in the Netherlands at the time of the Commonwealth.

The cathedral collection was originally made up of Latin Bibles, psalters and a valuable MS of old English romances collected by Robert Thornton. He donated his library to the cathedral in about 1430, and is buried in the building.

Sadly, between 1816 and 1826 all the Caxtons and many other early volumes were sold, with the proceeds going to purchase more modern books. The library flourishes today under the librarianship of Dr Nicholas Bennett. He is seen here with an early Old Testament that survived. It was copied before 1200.

++

The Capitall Lawes of *New-England*, as they ftand now in force in the Common-Wealth.

BY THE COVRT,

17

In the Years 1641. 1642.

Capitall Lawes, Eftablifhed within the Iurifdiction of *Maffachufets.*

1. IF any man after legall conviction, fhall have or worfhip any o'her God, but the Lord God, he fhall be put to death. *Deut.* 13. 6, &c. and 17. 2. &c. *Exodus* 22. 20.

2. IF any man or woman be a Witch, that is, hath or confulteth with a familiar fpirit, they fhall be put to death. *Exod.* 22. 18. *Lev.* 20. 27. *Deut.* 18. 10, 11.

3. IF any perfon fhall blafpheme the Name of God the Father, Sonne, or Holy Ghoft, with direct, expreffe, prefumptuous, or high-handed blafphemy, or fhall curfe God in the like manner, he fhall be put to death. *Lev.* 24. 15, 16.

4. IF any perfon fhall commit any wilfull murther, which is manflaughter, committed upon premeditate malice, hatred, or cruelty, not in a mans neceffary and juft defence, nor by meer cafualtie, againft his will ; he fhall be put to death. *Exod.* 21. 12, 13, 14. *Num.* 35. 30, 31.

5. IF any perfon flayeth another fuddenly in his anger, or cruelty of paffion, he fhall be put to death. *Num.* 35. 20, 21. *Lev.* 24. 17.

6. IF any perfon fhall flay another through guile, either by poyfonings, or other fuch divilifh practice ; he fhall be put to death. *Exod.* 21. 14.

7. IF a man or woman fhall lye with any beaft, or bruit creature, by carnall copulation, they fhall furely be put to death ; and the beaft fhall be flaine, and buried. *Lev.* 20. 15, 16.

8. IF a man lyeth with mankinde, as he lyeth with a woman, both of them have committed abomination, they both fhall furely be put to death. *Lev.* 20. 13.

9. IF any perfon committeth adultery with a married, or efpoufed wife, the Adulterer, and the Adulterefle, fhall furely be put to death. *Lev.* 20. 10. and 18. 20. *Deut.* 22. 23, 24.

10. IF any man fhall unlawfully have carnall copulation with any woman-childe under ten yeares old, either with, or without her confent, he fhall be put to death.

11. IF any man fhall forcibly, and without confent, ravifh any maid or woman that is lawfully married or contracted, he fhall be put to death. *Deut.* 22. 25. &c.

12. IF any man fhall ravifh any maid or fingle woman (committing carnall copulation with her by force, againft her will) that is above the age of ten yeares ; he fhall be either punifhed with death, or with fome other grievous punifhment, according to circumftances, at the difcretion of the Judges : and this Law to continue till the Court take further order.

13. IF any man ftealeth a man, or man-kinde, he fhall furely be put to death. *Exod.* 21. 16.

14. IF any man rife up by falfe witneffe wittingly, and of purpofe to take away any mans life, he fhall be put to death. *Deut.* 19. 16. 18, 19.

15. IF any man fhall confpire, or attempt any invafion, infurrection, or publick rebellion againft our Common-wealth, or fhall indeavour to furprize any Towne or Townes, Fort or Forts therein : or fhall treacheroufly, or perfidioufly attempt the alteration and fubverfion of our frame of pollity, or government fundamentally, he fhall be put to death. *Num.* 16. 2 *Sam.* 3. & 18. & 20.

Per exemplar Incre, Nowel, Secret.

Printed firft in *New-England*, and re-printed in *London* for *Ben. Allen* in *Popes-head Allen.* 1 6 4 3.

One book that has left the library is *The Capital Laws of New England*, which in 1641 was part of the Commonwealth. In 1955 the book was auctioned on behalf of the cathedral in Boston, USA. It raised £3,570 14s 2d.

There are some interesting seals in the cathedral. This is the silver matrix, which depicts the Blessed Virgin Mary (to whom the cathedral is dedicated) holding the infant Jesus.

The infamous Lincoln Imp. He is to be found at the top of the last complete column on the north side of the angel choir. This impression of him is less accurate than the picture on the next page.

Many Lincoln churchmen have wanted to ban the Imp as a symbol of Lincoln. Perhaps it is intended to serve as a reminder that evil is always present. The Imp wanted to 'knock over his Lordship [the bishop] and blow up the Dean, Organist and singers, knock out the windows and put out the lights' in the cathedral. One could argue that the administrative upheavals of the late 1980s and early 1990s almost allowed the Imp to achieve his goal, but thankfully this has not been the case.

There are hundreds of gargoyles and curious carvings all over the cathedral. This example of Bacchus is a boss at the north-west angle of vaulting of the lantern under the centre tower.

Of all the gargoyles, this one on the west front appears to have the most demented expression.

This monkey has lost his face.

This creature in the cloisters could almost have come straight out of a Gerald Scarfe cartoon.

This fine statue of Edward I and Queen Eleanor is on the south-east corner of the building.

In the Middle Ages pilgrims from far and wide used to visit Lincoln Cathedral to pray.

The statue of Bishop Hugh of Avalon (St Hugh of Lincoln), bishop from 1186 to 1200, on the south-west pinnacle. This likeness of him is reputedly the best in existence. Virtually the whole cathedral, except the angel choir and part of the transepts, was of Hugh's design – but he did not live to see all the work completed.

ST. HUGH.

From the S. W. Pinnacle of Lincoln Cathedral.

Probably the best likeness in existence Erected A.D. 1200.

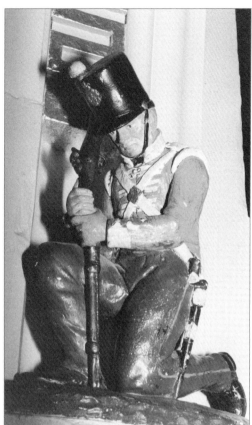

These two models guard the entrance to St George's chapel, off the north transept. They look like tin soldiers. The one on the right is dressed in the uniform of the Lincolnshire Crimean War Regiment (1847–57) while the figure below is of a First World War private, with his rifle pointing down as a mark of respect.

The famous Tennyson statue on Minster Green, which was carved by the poet laureate's old friend G.F. Watts RA. Sadly Watts died before the unveiling.

Bishop Richard Fleming's unusual monument, in the Fleming Chantry, has the stone figure of a skeleton in a shroud just underneath it. Bishop Fleming died in 1430. One of his lasting achievements was to found Lincoln College, Oxford.

This is the Easter Sepulchre, erected in about 1310 on the north side of the high altar, with the remains of Bishop Remigius buried next to it. Remigius's coffin measured 51 by 16 in; he was described as 'little of stature, but great of heart; dark complexion, but fair in deeds'.

Not all the tombstones in the cathedral are elaborate. George Stowell's epitaph simply reads: 'Clockwinder 1960–1980'.

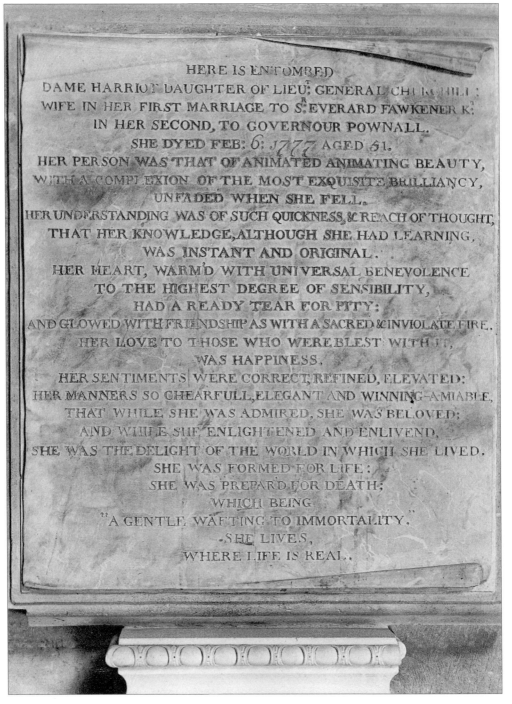

HERE IS ENTOMBED
DAME HARRIOT DAUGHTER OF LIEU: GENERAL CHURCHILL :
WIFE IN HER FIRST MARRIAGE TO S: EVERARD FAWKENER K:
IN HER SECOND, TO GOVERNOUR POWNALL.
SHE DYED FEB: 6: 1777 AGED 51.
HER PERSON WAS THAT OF ANIMATED ANIMATING BEAUTY,
WITH A COMPLEXION OF THE MOST EXQUISITE BRILLIANCY,
UNFADED WHEN SHE FELL.
HER UNDERSTANDING WAS OF SUCH QUICKNESS, & REACH OF THOUGHT,
THAT HER KNOWLEDGE, ALTHOUGH SHE HAD LEARNING,
WAS INSTANT AND ORIGINAL.
HER HEART, WARM'D WITH UNIVERSAL BENEVOLENCE
TO THE HIGHEST DEGREE OF SENSIBILITY,
HAD A READY TEAR FOR PITY:
AND GLOWED WITH FRIENDSHIP AS WITH A SACRED & INVIOLATE FIRE.
HER LOVE TO THOSE WHO WERE BLEST WITH IT,
WAS HAPPINESS.
HER SENTIMENTS WERE CORRECT, REFINED, ELEVATED:
HER MANNERS SO CHEARFULL, ELEGANT AND WINNING-AMIABLE,
THAT WHILE SHE WAS ADMIRED, SHE WAS BELOVED;
AND WHILE SHE ENLIGHTENED AND ENLIVEND,
SHE WAS THE DELIGHT OF THE WORLD IN WHICH SHE LIVED.
SHE WAS FORMED FOR LIFE :
SHE WAS PREPARD FOR DEATH;
WHICH BEING
"A GENTLE WAFTING TO IMMORTALITY,"
SHE LIVES,
WHERE LIFE IS REAL.

Of all the memorial inscriptions in the cathedral, the one for Dame Harriet Churchill, daughter of Lt.-Gen. Churchill, must rank as one of the most flattering. Dame Harriet married Sir Everard Fawkener first, and subsequently 'Governour' Pownall. She is described as having 'a complexion of the most exquisite brilliance unfaded when she fell' and 'animating beauty', together with a 'heart warmed with universal benevolence'. Moreover, 'her sentiments were correct, refined and elevated', and 'her manners were elegant'.

This lectern, given in memory of Dean Butler, now sadly lies in storage.

The ornate pulpit, attributed to Sir Christopher Wren, was given to the cathedral in 1913. It was rescued from the Anglican church of St Mary, Rotterdam, Holland, which was then under renovation. It was donated by A.C. Benson in memory of his father, Edward White Benson, once Chancellor of Lincoln, after which he was Bishop of Truro and finally Archbishop of Canterbury.

The choir stalls were considered by Pugin to be the finest in the country. This photograph was taken in about 1963; in the foreground are some sixth form boarders from Lincoln School.

There is no need for this 'improvement': the spikes over St Hugh's headshrine are ugly and incongruous. Geoffrey Clarke's stained glass windows in the treasury are dull, in my opinion, but Duncan Grant's mural in the Russell chantry is sensitive.

There is even a 'Lincoln Cathedral' rose!

CATHEDRAL PEOPLE

The diocesan readers at their annual festival in Lincoln Cathedral, 24 September 1949.

Over the years many characters have been associated with the cathedral. Pictured here is Canon H.W. Hutton, who lived in Vicars' Court from 1880 to 1916. He had many interests outside the cathedral including the Bromhead Hospital: his wife's maiden name was Bromhead, so it is likely that the hospital had been founded by her family.

Another character was Canon Charles Harold Scott, who was a priest vicar in 1901 and died in 1940. Like Hutton, he was a resourceful cleric.

Casting sheet lead for the cathedral roof, January 1946. Canon Larken is looking on. In total there are 550 tons of lead on the roof, covering an area of 3¼ acres.

The chancellors of Lincoln included Chancellor Crowfoot (1893–1913).

He was succeeded by the Rev. Octavius Johnstone (1913–23).

Chancellor Kaye (1863–1913), son of Bishop Kaye, served the cathedral for fifty years. His memorial plaque is just outside the canons' vestry.

He was followed by Canon Jeudwine, archdeacon from 1913 to 1925 and sub-dean from 1929 to 1933.

The Venerable A. Clifford Jarvis, archdeacon of Lincoln and residentiary canon of the cathedral, retired in 1971. He devoted much of his time to the preservation of old churches and parsonages.

Canon Cook was appointed sub-dean in 1946, and served until 1961. This portrait is by the late Margaret Dudding, and was an excellent likeness of him.

Dean Butler (1885–94) outside the north-west cloister wrought-iron gate.

Dean Wickham (1894–1910), who married Agnes, the daughter of Prime Minister William Gladstone, in 1873.

Probably the most dynamic dean Lincoln ever had was Thomas Charles Fry, whose fund-raising efforts between 1910 and 1930 (when he was dean) saved the cathedral from collapse.

The Rt. Rev. Colin Dunlop, Dean of Lincoln
from 1949 to 1964, was the only bishop ever to
be made a dean of Lincoln.

He was succeeded by Dean Peck, who was
installed on 29 January 1965, but sadly died in
April 1968. Here we see his installation.

The installation of Dean Oliver Twisleton Wickham Fiennes, 24 January 1969. Oliver Fiennes' distant cousin is Sir Ranulph, the Arctic explorer. In the foreground of this picture is David Rutter, while on the left is Ted Mason, the chapter clerk.

Edward King, bishop from 1885 to 1910, was responsible for moving the bishop's palace from Riseholme to the neighbourhood of the cathedral. Edward King House, as it is now called, serves as an ecumenical centre and offers bed and breakfast facilities.

This photograph of Bishop Swayne was taken at
Crowland Abbey amongst the ruins. Swayne
was bishop from 1920 to 1932.

Bishop Nugent Hicks, formerly the Bishop of
Gibraltar, was Bishop of Lincoln from 1933 to
1942.

The enthronement of any bishop is a solemn commitment. Here we see Bishop Leslie Owen's enthronement in 1946. Sadly Owen was a sick man when he took office, and was dead within a year.

He was followed by Bishop Harland, seen here arriving for his enthronement in 1947. Dean Mitchell is on the right.

The enthronement of Kenneth Riches, 1956.

Bishop Riches is seen here at the confirmation of some choristers, when Tim Hine was the succentor.

It was Bishop Greaves who paved the way for the return of the choir school from Lincoln School on Wragby Road back to the cathedral precincts in 1963. Arthur Ivan Greaves (1873–1959) was precentor of Lincoln Cathedral from 1937 to 1958. (He was also Bishop of Grantham in 1935 and Bishop of Grimsby from 1937 to 1958.)

In 1975 Simon Phipps was enthroned. He is seen here with Dean Oliver Fiennes.

This is a particularly pleasing picture of Bishop Simon and Mary Phipps walking in the garden, 1975.

This is a much more formal group shot of Adelbert Devaux after accepting a prebendal stall which is reserved for him in the choir of the cathedral, 17 November 1983. He was a Roman Catholic priest in the diocese of Bruges, Belgium. Left to right: Amos Lunn (verger), Cecil Jollands (chapter clerk), an assistant priest, Canon Adelbert Devaux, the Rt. Rev. Simon Phipps (bishop), Derek Wellman (diocesan registrar), Canon Graham Neville (1982–7).

There can be no doubt that the choir is one of the finest cathedral choirs in the country. It is seen here in Dean Dunlop's time, *c.* 1956.

The choir, *c.* 1965. Also pictured are Charles Carter (head verger 1964–72), Harold A. Bunyan (verger 1958–66), John Taylor (verger 1968–78), the Rev. Paul Appleton (succentor 1960–85), the Rev. David W. Tweddle (priest vicar 1963–5), and in the centre Bishop Dunlop.

The cathedral choir, *c.* 1969.

There was a choir school at the cathedral for hundreds of years, but it was disbanded during the First World War. In 1919 choristers were sent to Lincoln School (on Wragby Road) to mix with other pupils, and the choir school only returned to the cathedral in 1963.

In the 1930s the choir school had its own cricket team.

It also had a football team.

Here we see Dr Gordon Slater, organist and master of the choristers from 1930 to 1967, conducting the Lincoln Musical Society annual concert of 1959, held in the Corn Exchange on 25 November. In this performance of *Dido and Aeneas* by Henry Purcell, the soloists were Eileen Poulter (soprano), Iris Bourne (soprano), Jean Graystone (contralto) and Gordon Clinton (baritone). The Lemare Orchestra was led by Lawrence Turner.

Dr Gordon Slater was appointed organist and choirmaster of Boston parish church in 1919. In 1927 he went to Leicester Cathedral, and was appointed at Lincoln in 1930. Dr Slater trained under Sir Edward Bairstow, and continued the traditions set down by Dr G. J. Bennett, his predecessor.

Philip Marshall, organist and master of the choristers, retired in 1985. He was followed by David Flood, who returned to Canterbury, and Colin Walsh, the present organist. Perhaps their most illustrious predecessor was William Byrd, England's foremost composer during the reigns of Elizabeth I and James I, and organist of Lincoln from 1563 to 1572. His memorial tablet is in the north choir aisle.

Clifford Hewis was a chorister at Lincoln from 1921 to 1926, and became assistant organist from 1931 to 1975. He was also music master at Lincoln School.

The cathedral staff is made up of many individuals who all contribute to the day-to-day maintenance, administration and general upkeep of the building. This is the late William Barratt OBE, head verger. In service life with the Royal Navy, the Duke of Edinburgh had served under Captain William Barratt, and when he visited the cathedral with the Queen in 1958 he spotted Barratt straight away.

Another character was Albert Richardson, gardener and boiler stoker, who occasionally used to bathe his children in a tin bath in the boiler room on Sunday morning during Matins, unbeknown to worshippers.

Harold Spencer was the cathedral engineer, and worked for the dean and chapter for nearly half a century. This photograph was taken in 1982, and shows him at work on a lathe, kindly donated to the cathedral by the famous Ruston Gas Turbines.

Sir Francis Hill (left) and Sir Harold Banwell (second left) in Vicars' Court. Sir Francis Hill was Lincoln's best-known historian and together with Banwell served on the Fabric Fund of Lincoln Cathedral.

The chapter clerk, Cecil Jollands, and his two assistants, Ann Thomas and Dianne Loynes.

Lawrence Bond was appointed architect in 1958 to oversee any structural alterations. In this photograph, dating from 1963, Bond (the gentleman on the right) is looking over the parapet together with the clerk of the works, J.A. Higgins. Bond was also the architect for Salisbury Cathedral and Newark parish church. He died in 1993 aged eighty-four.

Bob Hellowell, who also happened to be a lay vicar, was part of the restoration team in the 1960s. Here he is working on a stained glass window.

Leslie Fagg and Norman Bonner carve some timbers in the roof space. They are using an air motored saw which does not create sparks, and eliminates fire hazard.

Many famous people have visited the cathedral, such as Sir Alec Rose in 1969. He is seen here with Canon Peter Binnall admiring the bell of HMS *Tasman* in the seamen's chapel.

The wedding of Michael Adie's daughter Kate, *c.* 1981; Simon Phipps officiated. Adie, who was rector of Louth, archdeacon of Lincoln from 1977 to 1983 and latterly Bishop of Guildford, had his portrait painted by Antony Williams. This portrait gained Williams the commission to paint Queen Elizabeth II, with the famous 'hands' that so shocked the public. The other bishops present here are David Stewart Cross, Bishop of Blackburn, and Simon Burrows, Bishop of Buckingham.

Rex Davies was originally employed as Warden of Edward King House, and later became sub-dean.

Magna Carta was granted by King John at Runnymede in 1215. It has often been seen as a basically democratic document, protecting the people from excessive royal power. Four original copies of Magna Carta still exist: two are lodged at the British Library, while the other two are held by Salisbury and Lincoln cathedrals.

In recent years Lincoln's Magna Carta has been used to raise much-needed funds. A tour of America, arranged by Dean Oliver Fiennes, was very successful, but perhaps the less said about the follow-up tour of Australia the better. This photograph shows Jackie Osgodby, cathedral shop assistant, with a copy of the Magna Carta – facsimiles of which are available for purchase in the shop, together with a wide range of cathedral prints.

MAINTENANCE & RESTORATION

Prince Charles visited the cathedral in 1979. He was given a fairly extensive tour of the restoration work that was being carried out.

Victorian reconstruction of the path and roadway outside the Galilee porch on the south side of the cathedral.

A new pavement replaced the Victorian work in 1984.

During the twentieth century the most pressing problem has been the upkeep of this fine Gothic pile. This was photographer 'Sammy' Smith's view of the west front before restoration began.

Over the years a combination of weather and pollution has taken its toll. Victorian and Edwardian industrialisation had left its mark in more ways than one. But the most urgent problem was that the cathedral had never been repaired after the great earthquake of 1185, and the once-small cracks and holes were now posing some very serious questions. This photograph dates from 1917.

Robert Godfrey's plans of the north-west tower, dated 10 June 1932. The note reads: 'The zig-zag lines indicate the exact position of the fractures prior to the special repairs.'

By the 1920s the dean and chapter had realised the enormity of the task ahead of them. Work was started in 1922 and continued for ten years.

Sam Smith took many photographs to chart the work in progress. This photograph of the judgement porch was taken before the statue of the Blessed Virgin and Child was placed between the two arches.

Taken from Alfred Shuttleworth's house in Eastgate (now the Eastgate Hotel), this photograph shows scaffolding being erected around the central tower.

Eventually the tower was completely enveloped. This was the scene in May 1931.

Hardly a stone of the cathedral missed inspection. St Hugh's statue stands on the top of the pinnacle that has been engulfed in scaffolding.

On 16 August 1932 Dean Robert Mitchell and Sub-Dean Canon Jeudwine laid the head of the cross on the south-west transept gable parapet. Also in the photograph are Priest Vicar Foster, Robert Godfrey, J. Tebbs, A. Freestone, P. Joyce and the verger, Mr Welbourn.

A nave altar was specially relocated for the thanksgiving service for the completion of the 'special repairs' (as they had been known), which took place on 3 November 1932. A young Duke and Duchess of York (later to become George VI and Queen Elizabeth) attended the service.

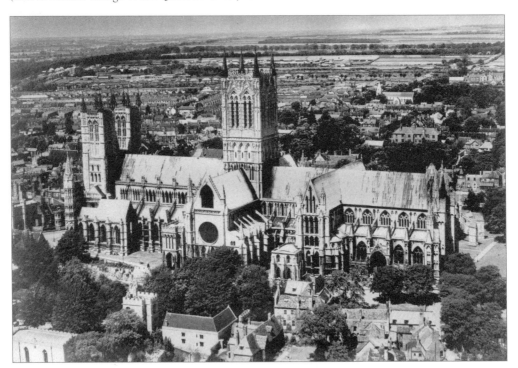

This is how the cathedral looked after the first major restoration. The Ermine Estate was yet to be built.

Once the outside was completed, restoration started on the inside of the cathedral. These works were carried out between November 1936 and January 1937. The scaffolding was cleared away in May that year.

The angel choir was in particular need of repair.

Many Lincolnians must have thought that the work would never cease.

Robert S. Godfrey, surveyor and clerk of the works, originally came to the cathedral in 1902. He was appointed clerk of the works in 1916 and was subsequently awarded a CBE and finally a Lambeth MA. During his career as surveyor he strengthened, and on two occasions saved, vital parts of the building's structure. This photograph was taken in July 1931.

Here we see Robert Godfrey pointing out some of the problems in the east window of the angel choir, 1935. Godfrey carefully catalogued all the work that was undertaken, and these records are a good foil to Sam Smith's photographs. Smith left hundreds of photographs of this period in the cathedral's history.

If there were problems inside there were also problems outside. This shows the timbers that were needed to support the buttresses.

The east end wall had split away from the north and south walls. It was only secured by drilling holes of between 20 and 40 ft deep, then inserting bronze bars, and finally injecting liquid cement under high pressure; this held everything together.

The caption on this photograph might have been: 'Bert, I wish these blessed railings weren't in the way!' These workmen were drilling holes at the east end in July 1935.

In 1937 a few examples of the damaged stonework found in the angel choir were put on show.

One of the best ways of cleaning stone is with a high-pressure hose, and when Walter Toynbee tried this method during the 1920–32 restoration it must have been revolutionary.

It must not be forgotten that all this work was made possible through the untiring efforts of Dean T.C. Fry, pictured here in Bedford Hills, New York, while on one of his fund-raising missions.

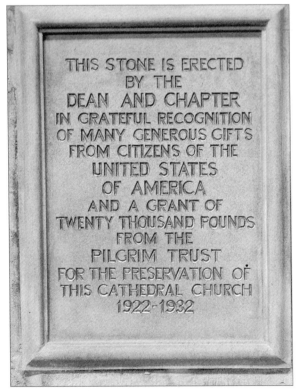

THIS STONE IS ERECTED
BY THE
DEAN AND CHAPTER
IN GRATEFUL RECOGNITION
OF MANY GENEROUS GIFTS
FROM CITIZENS OF THE
UNITED STATES
OF AMERICA
AND A GRANT OF
TWENTY THOUSAND POUNDS
FROM THE
PILGRIM TRUST
FOR THE PRESERVATION OF
THIS CATHEDRAL CHURCH
1922-1932

Eventually a stone plaque was erected inside the cathedral to acknowledge all the donations that had made the work possible.

Despite the major works of the 1920s and '30s restoration had to go on. Fred Higgins is seen here inspecting rotten timbers in 1963.

Even unexpected repairs had to be taken into account. In June 1970 a disused flue caused the collapse of masonry on the gable end of what was the Sub-Deanery.

Repairs to the cathedral were to be an ongoing expense. The electrical system needed rewiring, and Fred Higgins is seen here showing the electrician where to route the wires.

In 1980 Fred Higgins was awarded a BEM for his services as clerk of works. Sir Henry Neville presented the medal to him in a private ceremony at the Higgins's home; Canon John Nurser (Chancellor) is looking on.

One of the most dangerous tasks is removing the weather vane on the central tower for cleaning. David Dawson (father) and Ian Dawson (son) of Dawson Steeplejacks, Bristol, are seen here on 13 April 1983.

EVENTS

The Lincoln Triennial Festival was held on 8 and 9 June 1910. It opened with an orchestral concert in the Corn Exchange, and the following afternoon Elgar conducted The Dream of Gerontius *in the cathedral. A group of the distinguished personalities taking part in the festival were photographed in the cathedral organist's back garden at North Place, Nettleham Road. Back row, left to right: Gervase Elwes (soloist), H.S. Trevitt (deputy cathedral organist), Rev. C.H. Scott (cathedral succentor), J.P. Rayner (hon. secretary), Charles Macpherson (sub-organist of St Paul's Cathedral), Sir Edward Elgar, Francis Harford (soloist). Front row: Miss Phyllis Lett (soloist), Miss Agnes Nicholls, Miss Carmen Hill, Dr G.J. Bennett (cathedral organist for thirty-five years, and founder of the Lincoln Musical Society in 1896).*

My favourite photograph of the 1920s would have to be Dean Fry pictured with a group of foreign dignitaries. They have all come prepared with umbrellas!

The crowning glory for Lincoln was the visit of the then Duke and Duchess of York, who attended the service of thanksgiving for the completion of the special repairs on 3 November 1932.

Crowds of people gathered to watch the royal couple leave the cathedral.

The cathedral had acted as a familiar landmark for the RAF. Once it was seen from the air many a pilot knew he was home. The cathedral built up a rapport with the RAF, and in May 1954 Sir George Mills, C-in-C of Bomber Command, unveiled the commemoration window in the RAF chapel. Facing left is Chancellor Milford.

The mayor's Christmas message was always delivered outside the west door on Christmas Eve. This is Mayor William Bell's message in 1955; he is accompanied by the Sheriff, Richard Grantham, and Bishop Harland.

In 1958 Queen Elizabeth visited Lincoln to open Pelham Bridge and also visited the cathedral. Here we see her leaving with Dean Colin Dunlop, and just behind them can be glimpsed Bishop Kenneth Riches with the Duke of Edinburgh. The mayor just visible in the background is Councillor Leslie Priestley.

When she was in the cathedral the Queen unveiled the Training Command window in the RAF chapel.

Sir John Barbirolli (1899–1970), conductor and cellist, conducted a concert on 30 July 1969 in Lincoln Cathedral: this proved to be his last concert appearance. He is seen here during rehearsal with members of the orchestra.

All musical evenings at the cathedral are well attended. This was the audience for Verdi's *Requiem*, 5 July 1971.

Sir David Willcocks was the conductor: this photograph shows the choir and part of the large orchestra.

To mark the ninth centenary of Lincoln
Cathedral (1072–1972) there was a
festival that included a performance of
Fauré's *Requiem*, a Grenadier Guards
march-past and the planting of the
cathedral vineyard. Discussing the
celebrations are Dean Oliver Fiennes
with the then MP for Lincoln, Dick
Taverne, who is now in the House of
Lords.

The Archbishop of Canterbury was present at the event. In this photograph the Most Rev. and Rt. Hon.
Michael Ramsey, with Mrs Ramsey just visible in the background, can be seen with Councillor Wilfred
Pixsley, Lincoln's mayor, and Dean Fiennes.

Herbert Howells (1892–1983), the composer,
shaking hands with Bishop Simon Phipps, 1975.
Howells is best known for his choral works, and
he composed the music for Simon Phipps'
enthronement.

Lincoln Cathedral has always maintained a high musical standard. This was a concert given on 15 June
1977 by the Royal Artillery Band.

Margaret Beckett, when she was Margaret Jackson and Lincoln's Labour MP, meets Bishop Simon Phipps at his enthronement, 18 January 1975.

The naturalist Dr David Bellamy and actress Susan Hampshire visited Lincoln to lecture at a conference entitled 'Population Concern' in 1977. They are seen here with Dean Oliver Fiennes, and the winner of a bicycle in the raffle.

Prince Charles conducted his usual informal walkabout, chatting to well wishers and admirers, when he visited the cathedral in 1979.

A tour of the cathedral included a visit to the mason's yard and workshop with Reg Godley, works manager, and Dean Oliver Fiennes. Ron James is the stonemason at work.

In 1980 Queen Elizabeth was back again. This time it was to celebrate the seven hundredth anniversary of the building of the angel choir. She is seen here arriving with Dean Fiennes. In the foreground is Archie Keighley (dean's verger) leading the procession.

When she left in the company of the Lord Lieutenant Henry Neville it was still raining.

Col. Clive Auchinleck (nephew of the famous field marshal), director of the fabric fund, is seen here (centre) having just accepted a cheque for £375, raised by a twelve-hour ten-pin bowling marathon at RAF Scampton. Also seen here, receiving a framed drawing of the central building of the RAF Cranwell College as a memento of the event, is Air Commander E.G.P. Jeffery. Chapter Clerk Cecil Jollands is presenting the picture.

There was a re-enactment in 1972 of Wesley's famous visit to Lincoln Cathedral on horseback.

This is not the enthronement of another bishop, but a remake of *The Prisoner of Zenda*, filmed in 1984 and partly set inside the cathedral.

In this procession emerging from the entrance to Edward King House, the architecture of Lincoln blends in well with Anthony Hope's romantic adventure fantasy.

The annual Lincoln May festival, 1984. Archdeacon Canon Bill Dudman is crowning the May queen
outside the west door of the cathedral.

In 1985 BBC film crews were in Lincoln to produce a version of Dickens's *Oliver Twist*. Castle Hill Square
served as a setting for many of the street and market scenes.

Many Yarborough School pupils acted as extras. On the right is Sara Bonner.

One of Lincoln's most famous sons is Steve Race, responsible for many television and radio broadcasts, and seen here as guest speaker for Lincoln Rotary Club, 7 March 1986. Back row, left to right: Len Drew (junior vice-president), Cecil Jollands (president), David Wortley (district governor), Geoff Nelson (chairman), Barry Jackson (senior vice-president). Front row: Steve Race, Councillor Ida Campbell (mayor), Councillor Jock Campbell (city sheriff), Philip Race (president of Lincoln Rotary Club, and Steve's brother).

One controversial event in the cathedral was this version of the figures from the nativity at Christmas 1983, which replaced the conventional crib. It caused an uproar.

I much prefer the original crib, dating from 1955.

The cathedral attracts about 250,000 visitors a year – parties are always welcome, but not always the coaches!

Many visitors buy souvenirs from the cathedral shop. Some may see this commercialism as unwelcome, but it is only through visitors' generosity that the cathedral can continue to function from day to day.

A group shot of cathedral staff and volunteers with Dean Fiennes in the middle. All these people help, in many different ways, to cope with the upkeep of Lincoln Cathedral, and to oversee its survival into the next century and beyond. Without these people the cathedral would not survive.

ACKNOWLEDGEMENTS

A special note of thanks must go to Cecil Jollands for putting up with all my questions while researching this book. In fact this book was his idea, not mine, and I hope he can detect his own wry humour in these pages. I must also thank Cliff Smith of the *Lincolnshire Echo*, C.V. Middleton, Geoffrey Roe, Peter Sharp, Gus de Cozar and the late Leslie Hare for allowing me to reproduce photographs. Last but not least I would like to thank Dr Nicholas Bennett, whose knowledge of cathedral matters can only stem from a well-organised index system; and the Dean and Chapter who allowed me access to the Sam Smith photographic collection, which is housed in the cathedral.

BRITAIN IN OLD PHOTOGRAPHS

DERNEY

erney: A Second Selection B Bonnard

DFORDSHIRE

ord R Wildman
fordshire at Work N Lutt
on S Smith

RKSHIRE

nd Maidenhead M. Hayles &
B. Hedges
nd Slough J Hunter
nd Thatcham P Allen
nd Windsor B Hedges
denhead M Hayles
bury P Allen
ding P Southerton
ding: A Second Selection
Southerton
hurst and Crowthorne K Dancy
ingham R Wyatt

CKINGHAMSHIRE

ersham J Archer
nd Stony Stratford A Lambert
sbury R Cook
chley R Cook
kingham and District R Cook
on Keynes R Cook

MBRIDGESHIRE

C Jakes

ESHIRE

ncham J Hudson
shire Railways M Hitches
dle J Hudson
ster S Nicholls
y Aircraft R Sturtivant

YD

yd Railways M Hitches & J Roberts

DESDALE

esdale Ed. Lesmahagow Parish
fistorical Association

RNWALL

nd Padstow M McCarthy
nd Helston P Treloar
with J Holmes
nd Truro A Lyne
nish Coast, The T Bowden
outh P Gilson
er Fal Estuary, The P Gilson
ance and Newlyn J Holmes
St Mawgan K Saunders
er Fal P Gilson

MBRIA

vick and the Central Lakes J Marsh
Counties at Work J Marsh
on and the Solway Plain E Nelson

RBYSHIRE

nd Matlock D Barton
nd Ripley J Potton & J North
nd Staveley D Matthews
ourne and Dovedale M Winstone
y D Buxton

DEVON

Around Plymouth T Bowden
Around Seaton and Sidmouth T Gosling
Colyton and Seaton T Gosling
Dawlish and Teignmouth G Gosling
Devon Aerodromes K Saunders
East Devon at War T Gosling
Exeter P Thomas
Exmouth and Budleigh Salterton
T Gosling
From Haldon to Mid-Dartmoor T Hall
Honiton and the Otter Valley J Yallop
Kingsbridge K Tanner
RAF Chivenor D Watkins
Seaton, Lyme Regis and Axminster
T Gosling

DORSET

Around Blandford Forum B Cox
Around Gillingham P Crocker
Bournemouth M Colman
Bridport and the Bride Valley J Burrell &
S Humphries
Dorchester T Gosling
Poole A Norbury
Weymouth and Portland T Gosling

DURHAM/LAKE DISTRICT

Darlington G Flynn
Darlington: A Second Selection G Flynn
Durham at Work M Richardson
Durham People M Richardson
Houghton-le-Spring and Hetton-le-Hole
K Richardson
Houghton-le-Spring and Hetton-le-Hole:
A Second Selection K Richardson
Sunderland S Miller
Teesdale D Coggins
Teesdale: A Second Selection F P Raine
Weardale J Crosby
Weardale: A Second Selection J Crosby

DYFED

Aberystwyth and North Ceredigion
Ed. Dyfed Cultural Serv Dept
Haverfordwest Ed. Dyfed Cultural
Serv Deptt
Upper Tywi Valley Ed. Dyfed Cultural
Serv Dept

ESSEX

Around Grays B Evans
Braintree and Bocking at Work A Smith
Chadwell Heath D Hewson
Chelmsford J Marriage
Clacton-on-Sea K Walker
Rayleigh C Booty
Southend-on-Sea K Crowe
Waltham Abbey K N Bascombe
Witham J Palombi

**GLOUCESTERSHIRE &
COTSWOLDS**

Along the Avon from Stratford to
Tewkesbury J Jeremiah
Around Cirencester E Cuss
Cheltenham: A Second Selection
R Whiting
Cheltenham at War P Gill
Cirencester J Welsford

Forest, The Ed. Mullen
Gloucester Ed. J Voyce
Gloucester: From the Walwin Collection
J Voyce
North Cotswolds, The D Viner
North Gloucestershire at War P Gill
Severn Vale, The A Sutton
South Gloucestershire at War P Gill
Stonehouse to Painswick A Sutton
Stroud and the Five Valleys S Gardiner
Stroud and the Five Valleys: A Second
Selection S Gardiner
Stroud's Golden Valley S Gardiner
Stroudwater and Thames & Severn
Canals E Cuss
Stroudwater and Thames & Severn
Canals: A Second Selection E Cuss
Tewkesbury and the Vale of Gloucester
C Hilton
Thornbury to Berkeley J Hudson
Uley, Dursley and Cam A Sutton
Wotton-Under-Edge to Chipping
Sodbury A Sutton

GWYNEDD

Anglesey M Hitches
Around Llandudno M Hitches
Gwynedd Railways M Hitches
Vale of Conway, The M Hitches

HAMPSHIRE

Fairey Aircraft R Sturtivant
Farnborough J Gosney
Gosport J Sadden

HEREFORDSHIRE

Herefordshire A Sandford

HERTFORDSHIRE

Bishop's Stortford & Sawbridgeworth
W Wright
Hitchin A Fleck
Letchworth R Lancaster
St Albans S Mullins
Stevenage M Appleton

ISLE OF MAN

T. T. Races B Snelling

ISLE OF WIGHT

Around Ryde D Parr
Cowes D Parr
Newport D Parr

JERSEY

Jersey: A Third Selection R Lempriere

KENT

Around Gravesham R Hiscock
Around Tonbridge C Bell
Around Whitstable C Court
Bexley M Scott
Bromley, Keston and Hayes M Scott
Canterbury: A Second Selection D Butler
Chatham and Gillingham P MacDougall
Chatham Dockyard P MacDougall
Deal J Broady
Early Broadstairs and St Peter's before
1944 B Wootton
East Kent at War D Collyer

Eltham J Kennett
Folkestone: A Second Selection A Taylor
Folkestone: A Third Selection A Taylor
Goudhurst to Tenterden A Guilmant
Gravesend R Hiscock
Herne Bay J Hawkins
Lympne Airfield D Collyer
RAF Hawkinge R Humphreys
RAF Manston Ed. RAF Manston Historical
Club
RAF Manston: A Second Selection
Ed. RAF Manston Historical Club
Ramsgate and Thanet Life D Perkins
Romney Marsh E Carpenter
Sandwich C Wanostrocht
Tunbridge Wells M Rowlands
Tunbridge Wells II M Rowlands &
I C Beavis
Wingham, Adisham and Littlebourne
M A Crane

LANCASHIRE

Around Clitheroe C Rothwell
Around Garstang C Rothwell
Around Kirkham C Rothwell
Around Lancaster S Ashworth
Avro Aircraft R Jackson
Blackpool C Rothwell
Bury J Hudson
Chorley and District J Smith
East Lancashire at War N Dunnachie
Fairey Aircraft R Sturtivant
Fleetwood C Rothwell
Heywood J Hudson
Lancashire Coast, The C Rothwell
Lancashire North of the Sands J Garbutt,
L & J Marsh
Manchester Road and Rail Edward Gray
Lytham St Annes C Rothwell
North Fylde C Rothwell
Ormskirk & District M Duggan
Poulton-le-Fylde C Rothwell
Preston A Crosby
Radcliffe J Hudson
Rossendale B Moore & N Dunnachie
Salford E Gray
Southport J Smith

LEICESTERSHIRE

Around Ashby de la Zouch K Hillier
Changing Face of Leicester, The
P & Y Courtney
Melton Mowbray T Hickman
Leicester D Burton
Leicester at Work D Burton
River Soar, The I Keil
Stilton Cheese T Hickman
Vale of Belvoir T Hickman

LINCOLNSHIRE

Around Grimsby J Tierney
Around Louth D Cuppleditch
Around Skegness W Kime
Grantham M Knapp
Grimsby J Tierney
Grimsby Docks J Tierney
Lincoln D Cuppleditch
Scunthorpe D Taylor
Skegness W Kime
Vale of Belvoir T Hickman

LONDON

Acton *T & A Harper-Smith*
Around Whetstone *J Heathfield*
Barnes, Mortlake and Sheen *P Loobey*
Balham and Tooting *P Loobey*
Brixton and Norwood *J Dudman*
Crystal Palace, Penge and Anerley
  M Scott
Ealing and Northfield *R Essen*
Greenwich and Woolwich *K D Clark*
Hackney: A Second Selection *D Mander*
Hammersmith and Shepherds Bush
  J Farrell & C Bayliss
Hampstead to Primrose Hill *M Holmes*
Fairey Aircraft *R Sturdivant*
Islington *D Withett & V Hart*
Kensington and Chelsea *B Denny & C Starren*
Lewisham and Deptford: A Second
  Selection *J Coulter*
Marylebone and Paddington *R Bowden*
Royal Arsenal, The, Woolwich
  R Masters
Southwark *S Humphrey*
Stepney *R Taylor & C Lloyd*
Stoke Newington *M Manley*
Streatham *P Loobey*
Theatrical London *P Berry*
Uxbridge, Hillingdon and Cowley
  K Pearce
Wimbledon *P Loobey*
Woolwich *B Evans*

MONMOUTHSHIRE

Chepstow and the River Wye *A Rainsbury*
Monmouth and the River Wye
  Ed. Monmouth Museum

NORFOLK

Cromer & District *M Warren*
Great Yarmouth *M Teun*
Norfolk at War *N Storey*
North Walsham & District *N Storey*
Wymondham and Attleborough *P Yaxley*

NORTHAMPTONSHIRE

Around Stony Stratford *A Lambert*

NOTTINGHAMSHIRE

Arnold and Bestwood *M Spick*
Arnold and Bestwood II *M Spick*
Around Newark *T Warner*
Changing Face of Nottingham, The
  G Oldfield
Kirkby and District *F Ashley et al*
Mansfield *Old Mansfield Society*
Newark *T Warner*
Nottingham Yesterday and Today
  G Oldfield
Sherwood Forest *D Ottewell*
Vale of Belvoir *T Hickman*
Victorian Nottingham *M Payne*

OXFORDSHIRE

Around Abingdon *P Horn*
Around Didcot and the Hagbournes
  B Lingham

Around Henley-on-Thames *S Ellis*
Around Highworth & Faringdon
  G Tanner
Around Wallingford *D Beasley*
Around Wheatley *M Gunther*
Around Witney *C Mitchell*
Around Woodstock *J Bond*
Banburyshire *S Gray*
Burford *A Jewell*
Garsington *M Guntner*
Oxford: The University *J Rhodes*
Oxfordshire Railways: A Second
  Selection *L Waters*
Thame To Watlington *N Hood*
Wantage, Faringdon and the Vale
  Villages *N Hood*
Witney *T Worley*
Witney District *T Worley*

POWYS

Brecon *Brecknock Museum*
Welshpool *E Bredsdorff*

SHROPSHIRE

RAF Cosford *A Brew*
Shrewsbury *D Trumper*
Shrewsbury: A Second Selection
  D Trumper
Whitchurch to Market Drayton
  M Morris

SOMERSET / AVON

Around Keynsham and Saltford *B Lowe*
Around Taunton *N Chipchase*
Around Weston-Super-Mare *S Poole*
Bath *J Hudson*
Bridgwater and the River Parrett
  R Fitzhugh
Bristol *D Moorcroft*
The Changing Face of Keynsham *B Lowe
  & M Whitehead*
Chard and Ilminster *G Gosling*
Crewkerne and the Ham Stone Villages
  G Gosling
Frome *D Gill*
Mendips, The *C Howell*
Midsomer Norton and Radstock
  C Howell
Minehead *J Astell*
Somerton and Langport *G Gosling*
Taunton *N Chipchase*
Wells *C Howell*
Weston-Super-Mare *S Poole*

STAFFORDSHIRE

Around Leek *R Poole*
Around Rugeley *T Randall*
Around Stafford *J Anslow*
Around Tamworth *R Sulima*
Around Tettenhall and Codsall *M Mills*
Black Country Railways *N Williams*
Black Country Road Transport *J Boulton*
Black Country Transport: Aviation
  A Brew
Brierley Hill *S Hill*
Bushbury *A Chatwin*
Heywood *J Hudson*
Lichfield *H Clayton*

Pattingham and Wombourne *M Mills*
Sedgley and District *T Genge*
Smethwick *J Maddison*
Stafford *J Anslow & T Randall*
Staffordshire Railways *M Hitches*
Stoke-on-Trent *I Lawley*
Tipton *J Brimble & K Hodgkins*
Walsall *D Gilbert*
Wednesbury *I Bott*
West Bromwich *R Pearson*

SUFFOLK

Around Mildenhall *C Dring*
Around Woodbridge *H Phelps*
Ipswich: A Second Selection *D Kindred*
Lowestoft *I Robb*
Southwold to Aldeburgh *H Phelps*
Stowmarket *B Malster*
Suffolk at Work: Farming and Fishing
  B Malster

SURREY

Around Epsom *P Berry*
Cheam And Belmont *P Berry*
Croydon *S Bligh*
Farnham: A Second Selection *J Parratt*
Kingston *T Everson*
Richmond *Ed. Richmond Local
  History Society*
Sutton *P Berry*

SUSSEX

Around Crawley *M Goldsmith*
Around Haywards Heath *J Middleton*
Around Heathfield *A Gillet*
Around Heathfield: A Second Selection
  A Gillet
Around Worthing *S White*
Arundel and the Arun Valley *J D Godfrey*
Bishopstone and Seaford *P Pople*
Bishopstone and Seaford: A Second
  Selection *P Pople & P Berry*
Brighton and Hove *J Middleton*
Brighton and Hove: A Second Selection
  J Middleton
Crawley New Town *P Allen & J Green*
East Grinstead *N Dunnachie*
Hastings *P Haines*
Hastings: A Second Selection *P Haines*
High Weald, The *B Harwood*
High Weald: A Second Selection
  B Harwood
Horsham and District *T Wales*
Lancing and Sompting *P Fry*
Lewes *J Middleton*
RAF Tangmere *A Saunders*

TAYSIDE

Dundee at Work *J Murray*

WARWICKSHIRE

Along the Avon from Stratford to
  Tewkesbury *J Jeremiah*
Around Coventry *D McGrory*
Around Leamington Spa *J Cameron*
Around Leamington Spa II *J Cameron*
Around Warwick *R Booth*
Bedworth *J Burton*

Birmingham Railways *M Hitches*
Coventry: A Second Selection *D McC*
Nuneaton *S Clews*
Rugby *Rugby Local History
  Research Group*
Stourbridge *R Clarke*

WESTMORLAND

Kendal *M Duff*

WILTSHIRE

Around Amesbury *P Daniels*
Around Devizes *D Buxton*
Around Highworth *G Tanner*
Around Highworth & Faringdon
  G Tanner
Around Melksham *Ed. Melksham and
  District Historical Association*
Around Salisbury *P Daniels*
Around Wilton *P Daniels*
Around Wootton Bassett, Cricklade
  Purton *T Sharp*
Castle Combe to Malmesbury *A Wils*
Chippenham and Lacock *A Wilson*
Corsham & Box *A Wilson*
Marlborough: A Second Selection
  P Colman
Nadder Valley *R Sawyer*
Salisbury *P Saunders*
Salisbury: A Second Selection *P Dana*
Salisbury: A Third Selection *P Danie*
Swindon: A Third Selection *Ed. The
  Swindon Society*
Swindon: A Fifth Selection *B Bridgem*
Trowbridge *M Marshman*

WORCESTERSHIRE

Around Malvern *K Smith*
Around Pershore *M Dowty*
Around Worcester *R Jones*
Evesham to Bredon *F Archer*
Redditch and the Needle District
  R Saunders
Redditch: A Second Selection
  R Saunders
Tenbury Wells *D Green*
Worcester *M Dowty*
Worcester in a Day *M Dowty*
Worcestershire at Work *R Jones*

YORKSHIRE

Around Rotherham *A Munford*
Around Thirsk *J Harding & P Wyon*
Beverley *P Deans & J Markham*
Bridlington *I & M Sumner*
Holderness *I & M Sumner*
Huddersfield: A Second Selection
  H Wheeler
Huddersfield: A Third Selection
  H Wheeler
Leeds Road and Rail *R Vickers*
Otley & District *P Wood*
Pudsey *Pudsey Civic Society*
Scarborough *D Coggins*
Skipton and the Dales *Ed. Friends of
  Craven Museum*
Wakefield *C Johnstone*
Yorkshire Wolds, The *I & M Sumner*